D1567741

GET TO WORK!

SHOOTING FOR THE STARS WITH A
ROCKET SCIENTIST

Gareth Stevens
PUBLISHING

BY JOAN STOLTMAN

Please visit our website, www.garethstevens.com. For a free color catalog of all our high-quality books, call toll free 1-800-542-2595 or fax 1-877-542-2596.

Cataloging-in-Publication Data

Names: Stoltman, Joan.
Title: Shooting for the stars with a rocket scientist / Joan Stoltman.
Description: New York : Gareth Stevens Publishing, 2019. | Series: Get to work! | Includes index.
Identifiers: ISBN 9781538216750 (pbk.) | ISBN 9781538216743 (library bound) | ISBN 9781538216767 (6 pack)
Subjects: LCSH: Rockets (Aeronautics)–Juvenile literature. | Astronautics–Vocational guidance–Juvenile literature. | Aerospace engineering–Juvenile literature.
Classification: LCC TL850.S7585 2019 | DDC 629.1–dc23

Published in 2019 by
Gareth Stevens Publishing
111 East 14th Street, Suite 349
New York, NY 10003

Copyright © 2019 Gareth Stevens Publishing

Designer: Bethany Perl
Editor: Joan Stoltman

Photo credits: Cover, p. 1 Monkey Business Images/Shutterstock.com; pp. 1-24 (background) MaLija/Shutterstock.com; pp. 1-24 (rectangular banner) punsayaporn/Shutterstock.com; pp. 1-24 (stars) Audrius Birbilas/Shutterstock.com; p. 5 (rocket interior) Paul Mcerlane/Bloomberg/Getty Images; p. 5 (V-2) RikoBest/Shutterstock.com; pp. 6-18 (text box) LoveVectorGirl/Shutterstock.com; p. 7 Great Images in NASA/Wikipedia.org; p. 9 nd3000/Shutterstock.com; p. 11 (students) Joan B. Carnett/Popular Science/Getty Images; p. 11 (Saturn V) Everett Historical/Shutterstock.com; p. 13 (Soyuz) NASA/Wikipedia.org; p. 13 (International Space Station) NASA/Crew of STS-132/Wikipedia.org; pp. 15, 17 Pallava Bagla/Corbis/Getty Images; p. 19 Robert Laberge/Getty Images News/Getty Images; p. 20 Bill Ingalls/NASA/Flickr.com; p. 21 (balloon) lorenzo gambaro/Shutterstock.com; p. 21 (straw) Joy Tasa/Shutterstock.com; p. 21 (string) Olga Danylenko/Shutterstock.com; p. 21 (galaxy) NASA Images/Shutterstock.com; p. 21 (torn paper and tape) Flas100/Shutterstock.com.

Printed in the United States of America

CPSIA compliance information: Batch #CS18GS: For further information contact Gareth Stevens, New York, New York at 1-800-542-2595.

CONTENTS

Words in the glossary appear in **bold** type the first time they are used in the text.

WHAT'S A ROCKET SCIENTIST?

Have you always loved solving problems? Do you enjoy learning how and why things work? Are you interested in space and flight? Maybe you should be a rocket scientist!

Rocket scientists—who are really called aerospace **engineers**—use science and engineering to plan, **design**, and build objects that fly in the air around Earth and in outer space. These objects use a special kind of engine called a rocket. This kind of engine is powered by gases made from burning **fuel**.

V-2 ROCKET

Often, people use the word "rocket" for objects that have a rocket engine. The V-2 rocket was the first rocket that could reach space!

SCHOOL DAYS

To be a rocket scientist, you'll need to go to college—the school after high school—for 4 years to study engineering. Many rocket scientists continue to higher levels of study after college.

Engineering schools teach design, math, and many different kinds of science, such as **physics** and **chemistry**. School never really ends for a rocket scientist. You'll always need to know about the latest inventions and discoveries in your field. Rocket scientists work hard every day to figure out how to design and build better rockets.

WATCH A LAUNCH!

Have an adult help you find a video online of a recent or famous rocket taking off from Cape Canaveral at Kennedy Space Center in Florida. Many different kinds of rockets, including privately owned rockets, are sent into space from there!

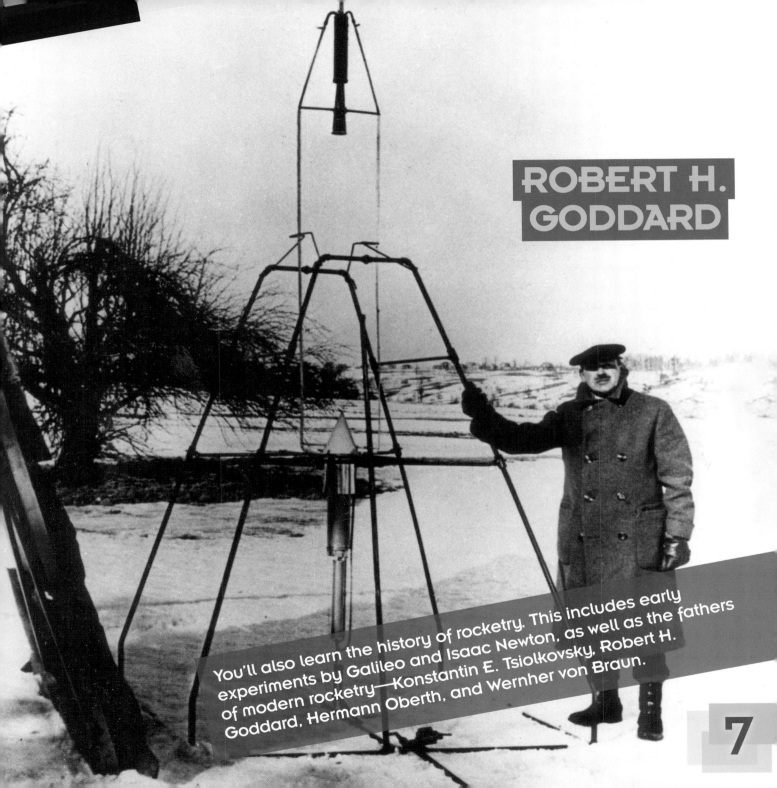

ROBERT H. GODDARD

You'll also learn the history of rocketry. This includes early experiments by Galileo and Isaac Newton, as well as the fathers of modern rocketry—Konstantin E. Tsiolkovsky, Robert H. Goddard, Hermann Oberth, and Wernher von Braun.

WHERE, OH, WHERE?

After college, rocket scientists work for at least 4 years as engineers in training while earning their engineering **license**. More than half of all aerospace engineers work in research and development. This means they study and invent new **materials** and methods to advance the field. Most other aerospace engineers make parts and **products**.

Most rocket scientists work for the government or for a private company that's been contracted, or hired, by the government. You can also work at an airplane or spacecraft company or work at a company that uses **satellites**.

Not all states have jobs for rocket scientists, though that's quickly changing. Recently, private companies have started to explore space. These companies include SpaceX, Orbital ATK, and Virgin Galactic.

9

NASA

When you think of NASA—the National Aeronautics and Space Administration—you probably picture an astronaut, right? However, about 60 percent of the people at NASA work in aerospace engineering!

Getting a job at NASA isn't easy. They don't hire often. Many jobs go to people who've worked at NASA for years in a contracted job. It helps to have hands-on **experience** with rockets and great grades. An **internship** at NASA while in college will likely get you hired after you finish school!

TAKE A TRIP!

Visit your local science museum or center. NASA has 11 education field centers outside these major cities: San Francisco and Los Angeles, California; Cleveland, Ohio; Washington, DC; Houston, Texas; Huntsville, Alabama; Orlando, Florida; and Biloxi, Mississippi.

SATURN V ROCKET

BLUE THUNDER

These students were part of a NASA **project** during college. Taking part in a project like this is a smart way to get NASA to hire you!

ROCKETS MAKE IT POSSIBLE

One of the coolest projects rocket scientists have ever been a part of is the International Space Station (ISS). Aerospace engineers and other scientists from 16 countries have been working together on this lab for many years now. They began construction in 1998, taking the lab into space in pieces using rockets. Today it's the size of two football fields, and astronauts live there year round!

A lab 250 miles (400 km) above Earth wouldn't be possible without many aerospace engineers working together, being creative, and thinking big!

THINK ABOUT IT!

Living on the ISS isn't easy. For example, salt has to be liquid, or it floats away! Write a list of your favorite things to eat. Think about how and if those things could be eaten in space. Do they need to be heated? Kept cold? Can you do that in space?

INTERNATIONAL SPACE STATION

SOYUZ ROCKET

Russia's Soyuz rockets have been used to fly people, supplies, and parts of the ISS into space over 950 times! US and Russian rockets make the ISS possible.

13

A DAY IN THE LIFE

Aerospace engineers can **specialize** in parts of a rocket, like fuel or air systems. Or they can be familiar with all the systems.

When a project is still just an idea, aerospace engineers decide *if* it's possible, how much it'll cost, and how long it'll take. Aerospace projects often take years—and can be stopped after years of work! Throughout building, rocket scientists test parts over and over—and sometimes invent new tests! After a project is built, aerospace engineers write directions and teach others how to use it.

Teams work on aerospace projects. A bigger project may even take many teams. Each team is in charge of certain parts. Because the parts will come together in the end, aerospace engineers keep the whole project in mind.

15

WHAT DOES IT TAKE?

A lot of people think you must be supersmart to be a rocket scientist. But it's actually more important to be creative, good at making decisions, and good at planning. You should also be able to solve problems and pay attention to even the smallest parts.

Of course, one of the most important skills rocket scientists need is to be good at teamwork! You have to work with a lot of different people to get even small projects done. Sometimes, you'll even need to lead a team!

TEST THAT LAW! PART 1

To build rockets, you must understand Newton's laws of motion. Newton's first law says that an object sitting still will stay still unless it's acted on by a force, and an object moving will keep moving unless it's acted on by a force.
If a shopping cart is sitting still on a flat floor, will it move? What if it's on a hill?

Aerospace engineer Pan Conrad once said, "You don't have to be good in math, you just have to stick with it. You don't have to be especially smart. You don't even have to be especially talented. You just have to be especially curious and you have to be dedicated."

INDIAN SPACE RESEARCH ORGANIZATION (ISRO) SCIENTISTS

THE WORLD NEEDS ROCKETS!

There are so many exciting things happening in the world of rocket science! NASA's New Frontiers program is all about exploring space farther than we've ever gone before. They're working on a powerful new kind of rocket that could make it possible to explore other worlds. There's even a Mars Exploration program that plans to land people on Mars in the 2030s!

But they need to invent the rockets to do that first! Will they be able to do it? Will you help them meet this goal?

TEST THAT LAW! PART 2

Newton's second law of motion says that heavier objects need more force to move the same distance as lighter objects. Push an empty shopping cart. Then push a loaded shopping cart. It takes more force to both push and stop the loaded shopping cart. Why?

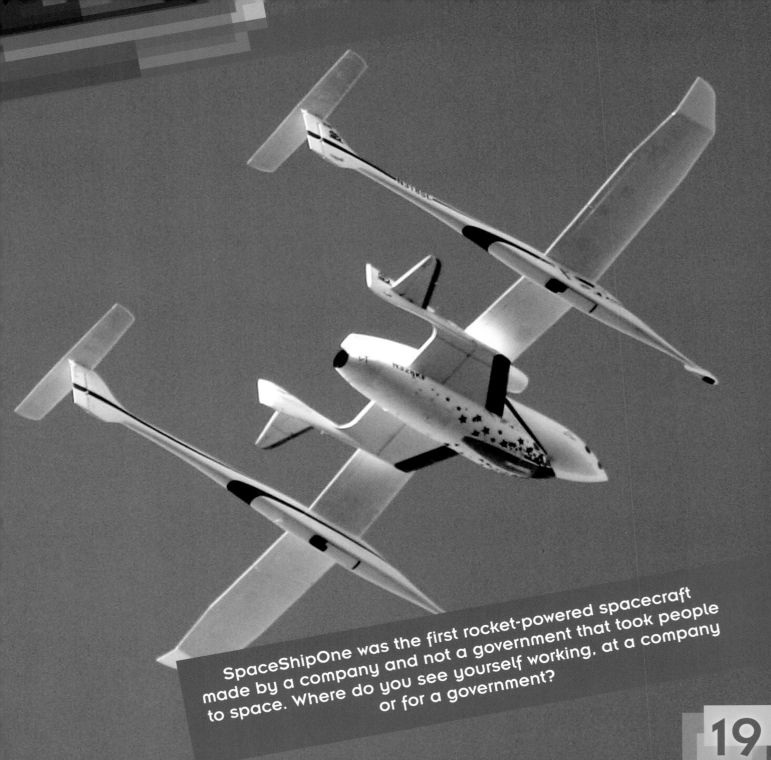

SpaceShipOne was the first rocket-powered spacecraft made by a company and not a government that took people to space. Where do you see yourself working, at a company or for a government?

19

READY?

Do you enjoy working on projects that take a while? Do you want to help the world? Do you dream of doing things that have never been done before? Do you pick yourself up and try again when you fail?

The cutting-edge field of rocket science needs dreamers and doers! It needs people who are willing to spend years trying and trying and trying again. If you look at the stars at night and get excited thinking about how much there is we don't know, then rocket science may be for you!

Understanding Newton's third law of motion is the key to rocketry. It says that for every action, there's an equal and opposite reaction. Rockets push a mixture of gases called exhaust out the back when they're on. This pushes the rocket forward!

BUILD A ROCKET!

YOU'LL NEED

- a ball of string
- a plastic straw
- tape
- scissors
- a balloon

LEVEL 1

1. Thread the string through the straw.
2. Attach each end of the string to the back of two chairs, stretching the line tightly.
3. Blow up a balloon and keep it tightly closed using your fingers.
4. Tape the balloon to the straw while still keeping it tightly closed.
5. Place the balloon near one end of the string with the open end closest to one chair.
6. Prepare to let go of the balloon with a countdown.
7. Let go of the balloon.

LEVEL 2

Use a much longer piece of string.

LEVEL 3

Make one end of the string higher.

LEVEL 4

Try different-sized and different-shaped balloons and different amounts of air.

GLOSSARY

chemistry: a science that deals with what matter is made of and with the changes matter can go through

design: the pattern or shape of something. Also, to create the pattern or shape of something.

engineer: someone who plans and builds machines. An aerospace engineer is someone who works on machines that travel into space.

experience: to gain skills and learning by doing something

fuel: matter such as coal, oil, or gas that is burned to make heat or power

internship: a period of time during school or after completing school when you work at a job to get experience and learn

license: an official paper that allows you to do, use, or have something

material: a type of matter from which something can be made

physics: a science that deals with matter and power and the way they act on each other in heat, light, sound, and electricity

product: something made or grown that is offered for sale

project: a planned piece of work that has a specific goal

satellite: a machine that is sent to space and that moves around Earth, the moon, sun, or another planet

specialize: to limit your work to one subject or thing to get really good at it

FOR MORE INFORMATION

Books

Labrecque, Ellen. *Yvonne Brill and Satellite Propulsion.* Ann Arbor, MI: Cherry Lake Publishing, 2017.

Lock, Deborah. *Rocket Science.* New York, NY: DK Publishing, 2015.

Waxman, Laura Hamilton. *Aerospace Engineer Aprille Ericsson.* Minneapolis, MN: Lerner Publications, 2015.

Websites

I Didn't Know That: How Rockets Work
video.nationalgeographic.com/video/i-didnt-know-that/idkt-how-rockets-work?source=relatedvideo
Watch this video all about rockets and Newton's third law of motion!

NASA Kids' Club
nasa.gov/kidsclub/index.html
This website is filled with games to play, pictures to see, videos to watch, and so much to read!

National Association of Rocketry Club Locator
www.nar.org/find-a-local-club/nar-club-locator/
Find a rocket club near you to see launches in person!

INDEX